Unstable Earth

What Happens when an ICE CAP Melts?

Angela Royston

A+
Smart Apple Media

Published by Smart Apple Media, an imprint of Black Rabbit Books
P.O. Box 3263, Mankato, Minnesota 56002
www.smartapplemedia.com

Published by arrangement with Wayland Books, London.

Cataloging-in-Publication Data is available from the Library of Congress
ISBN: 978-1-62588-160-1 (library binding)
ISBN: 978-1-62588-573-9 (eBook)

Picture Acknowledgements:
Dreamstime: Mrallen 9tr, Nouk 11t, Perx0955 8, Sugarfree.sk 7; FEMA: Ed Edahl 17; NASA Goddard Space Flight Center: Scientific Visualization Studio 4; Shutterstock: Ozerov Alexander 20-21, Avella 23b, Anton Balazh 22-23, boyan1971 18-19, Pichugin Dmitry 5, Peter Elvidge 21, Ewa Studio 6, Gentoo Multimedia Limited 13, Volodymyr Goinyk 25t, Jane A Hagelstein 12, irabel8 27b, JonMilnes 14, M.Khebra 26b, Yu Lan 28, LovelaceMedia 29, Patrick Poendl 26-27, Wyatt Rivard 10, Armin Rose 1, 24, Irina Schmidt 15, Thor Jorgen Udvang 16, 18, Gary Whitton 9l, Christian Wilkinson 25b, Jan Martin Will 3, 10-11.

Printed in the United States by CG Book Printers
North Mankato, Minnesota

PO 1730
3-2015

Contents

Meltdown

The Arctic and Antarctic are so cold that masses of thick ice, called **ice caps**, cover the sea and the land all year round. People used to take the ice caps for granted, but now they are beginning to melt. This book looks at what will happen as each ice cap disappears. This will affect the whole Earth and people everywhere.

When do ice caps melt the most?

Ice caps shrink in spring and summer as some of the ice melts, but they refreeze in winter. For thousands of years, the overall size of the ice caps has remained much the same. However, since 2000, things have begun to change dramatically.

More of the ice that covers the Arctic Ocean in winter is now melting in summer. This photograph was taken in August 2012. The orange line shows how much more ice there was at the end of summer in 2005.

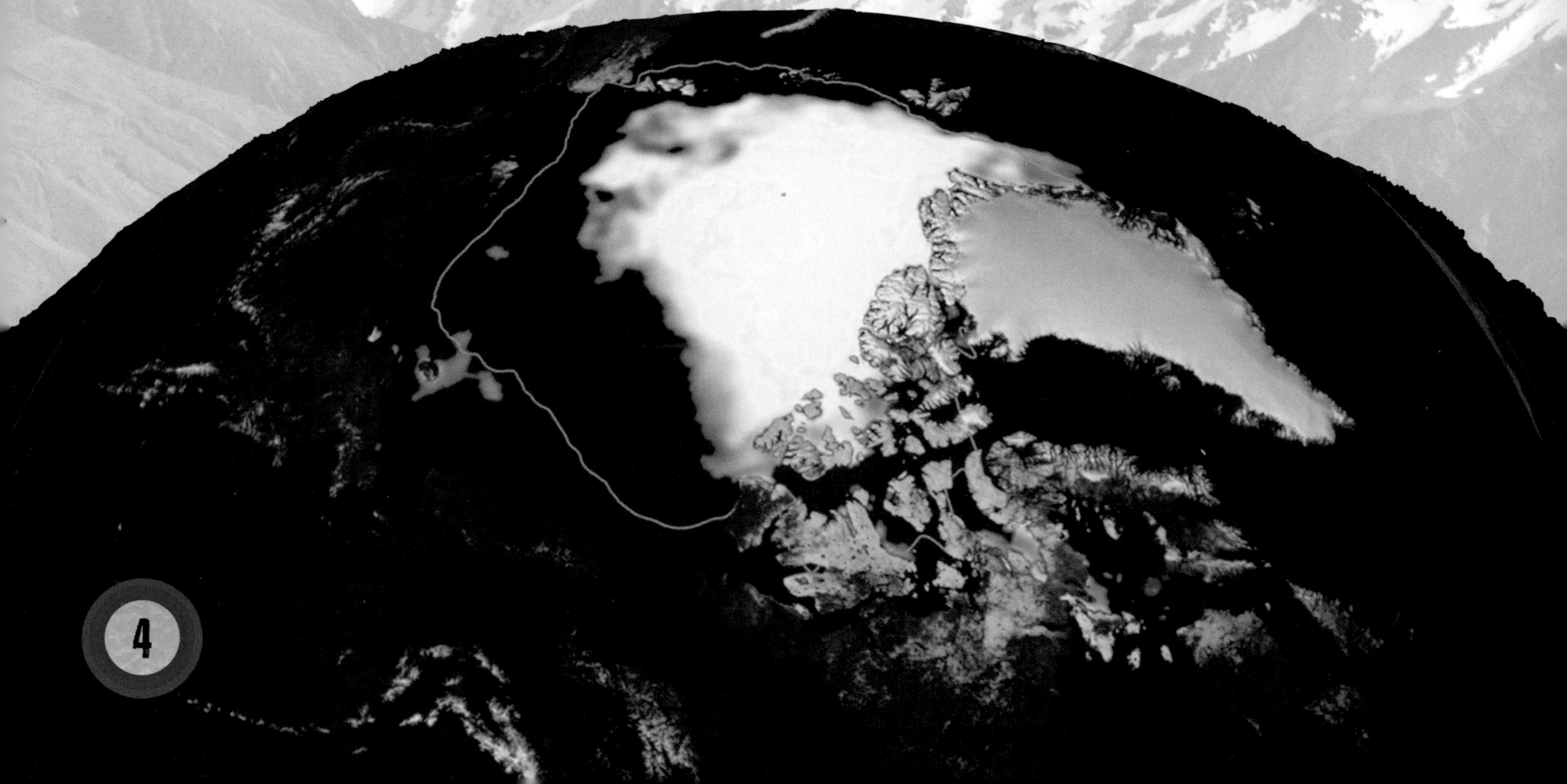

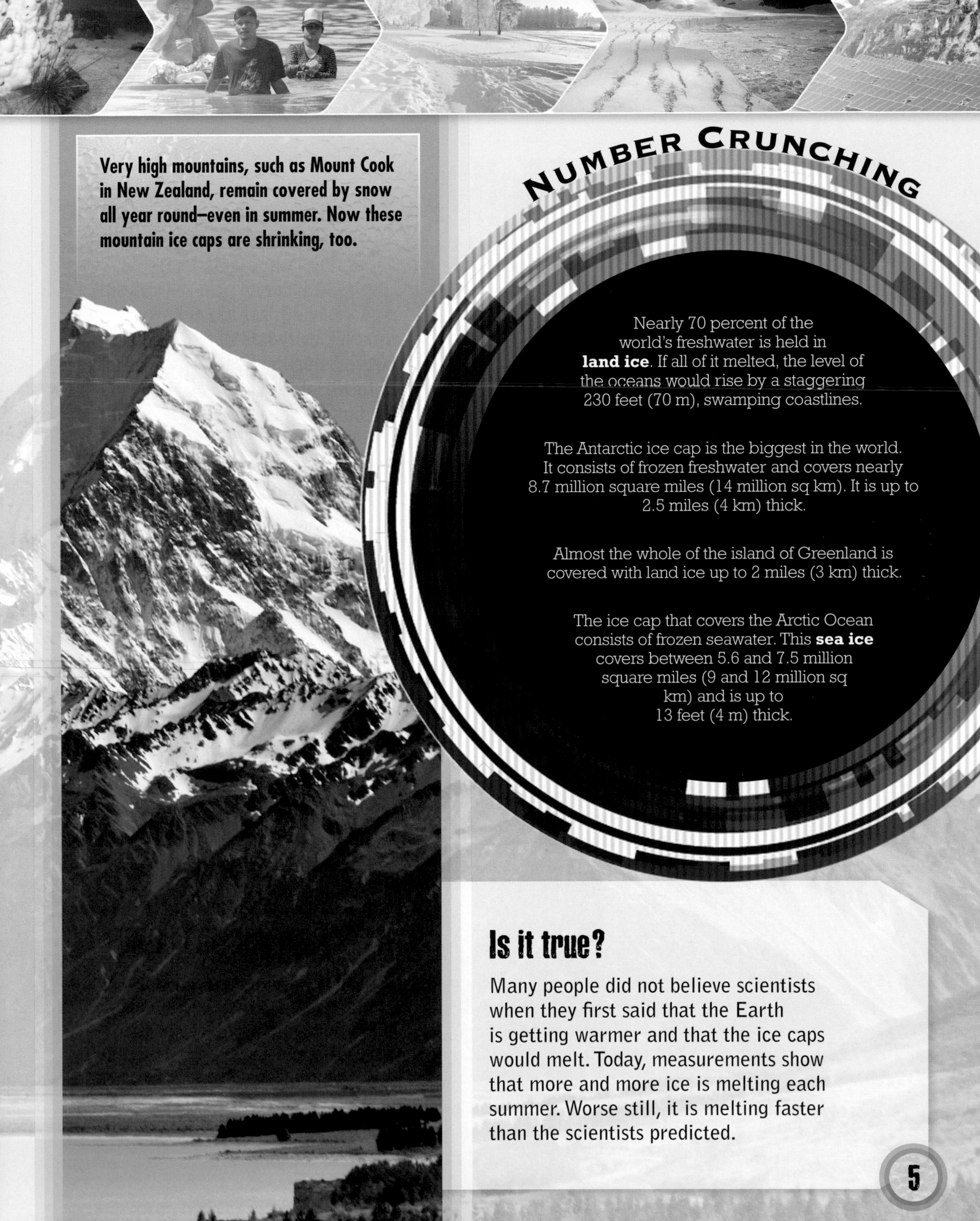

Very high mountains, such as Mount Cook in New Zealand, remain covered by snow all year round—even in summer. Now these mountain ice caps are shrinking, too.

Number Crunching

Nearly 70 percent of the world's freshwater is held in **land ice**. If all of it melted, the level of the oceans would rise by a staggering 230 feet (70 m), swamping coastlines.

The Antarctic ice cap is the biggest in the world. It consists of frozen freshwater and covers nearly 8.7 million square miles (14 million sq km). It is up to 2.5 miles (4 km) thick.

Almost the whole of the island of Greenland is covered with land ice up to 2 miles (3 km) thick.

The ice cap that covers the Arctic Ocean consists of frozen seawater. This **sea ice** covers between 5.6 and 7.5 million square miles (9 and 12 million sq km) and is up to 13 feet (4 m) thick.

Is it true?

Many people did not believe scientists when they first said that the Earth is getting warmer and that the ice caps would melt. Today, measurements show that more and more ice is melting each summer. Worse still, it is melting faster than the scientists predicted.

Why is the Ice Melting?

Polar ice is melting because the air at the surface of the Earth is getting warmer. This is called **global warming**. The pace of warming varies around the world, but the Arctic is warming six times faster than the average increase in temperature.

Have the ice caps melted before?

This is not the first time that the ice caps have melted. For example, 100 million years ago—when the dinosaurs lived—the world's **climate** was about 36° Fahrenheit (2° C) warmer than it is now. The current global warming is different, however. It is happening much faster, and the scientific evidence shows that it is humans who are causing it.

When ice melts, it reveals dark water and land. Dark surfaces absorb much more of the Sun's heat than white snow and ice.

An aircraft can travel a long way very fast. However aircraft burn vast quantities of fuel, and so create massive amounts of carbon dioxide and other greenhouse gases, which all contribute to global warming.

Heat trap

The Earth is becoming warmer because more of the Sun's heat is being trapped in the atmosphere. It is trapped by gases, particularly carbon dioxide and methane, which are known as greenhouse gases. Every year people produce billions of tons of **greenhouse gases** when they burn fossil fuels—coal, oil, and natural gas. They burn them, for example, to generate electricity and to run cars, aircraft, and other vehicles.

What happens next?

If we do not stop burning fossil fuels the temperature of the Earth will continue to rise. In that case, the first ice cap to melt will be the Arctic ice sheet.

⚠ Ice is white and reflects the Sun's heat. When the Arctic sea ice melts, the dark water below absorbs the Sun's heat and warms up. The warmer sea melts more ice.

⚠ The land around the Arctic Ocean is called the **permafrost** because it is permanently frozen. Now the permafrost is beginning to melt.

Melting Arctic

Fewer than ten years ago, scientists thought that it would take 60 years or more before the Arctic ice cap disappeared in summer. Many experts now expect the Arctic to be ice-free by 2020. This would open up new riches for the oil companies, but it is bad news for the Inuits and other people who live there.

Who gains if the ice melts?

Huge amounts of oil and gas are buried in rocks under the Arctic. In the past, these resources were out of reach, but now ships can sail through the Arctic in summer. The surrounding countries, particularly the United States, Canada, and Russia, have already laid claim to the oil. **Environmentalists** argue that it should be left in the rocks. They say that drilling to reach the oil will damage the environment for local people and animals.

The Inuit way of life is well adapted to life in an icy environment. Husky dogs are used to pull sleds across the ice and snow.

ON THE EDGE

The Inuit people, who have lived in the Arctic region for thousands of years, are now struggling to survive there. They are fighting the oil companies for their rights to the land. Their homes, which were built on solid, frozen ground, are now collapsing. As the permafrost melts, the buildings crack and slip on the soft ground below. In summer, the sea ice is now so thin that it is extremely dangerous to travel across.

Inuit children learn all the skills they need to survive on the ice lands in Greenland, Alaska, and northern Canada, but melting ice is threatening their way of life.

An oil **pipeline** snakes across the Alaskan countryside. Oil companies are planning to drill for more oil in the Arctic Ocean, where an oil spill would be catastrophic for local people and wildlife.

Increasing greenhouse gases

Burning the Arctic's oil will not only damage the local environment but it will also add to global warming. In addition, the **tundra** contains vast quantities of carbon dioxide and methane locked up in its permanently frozen ground. As the permafrost melts, these gases are released, adding further to global warming.

No Ice at the North Pole: Arctic 2025

Drilling for oil in the Arctic and transporting it in pipelines has disrupted the way of life of animals such as the **caribou**. It is hard for them to **migrate** across the tundra and to breed.

It is 2025. Governments have done little to stop global warming and the scientists' predictions have come to pass. The Arctic Ocean is ice-free in summer. The dark seawater soaks up the Sun's heat, adding to global warming. The permafrost is melting, releasing tons of extra greenhouse gases into the air.

WHERE WILL YOU BE IN 2025? IT'S YOUR FUTURE!

Inuits have been forced out of their villages and off their lands. They have had to leave their homes in the Arctic behind.

Consequences

Very few Inuits and other traditional people still live in the Arctic. Polar bears and many Arctic animals are almost extinct. Polar bears cannot survive the long, ice-free summers and are starving to death. They also have to compete with grizzly bears, gray wolves, and other animals that have moved north to take advantage of the warmer conditions in the Arctic.

This polar bear is stranded on a drifting sheet of ice. It has no hope of catching a seal in these open waters and may soon starve to death.

NEWS HEADLINES

A huge **oil slick** is spreading along the Arctic coast, killing wildlife. The oil spilled from an oil tanker, which collided with a container ship that was using the Arctic Ocean as a shortcut between the Atlantic and Pacific Oceans.

A dispute between Denmark and Canada over a tiny, uninhabited island off Greenland is turning ugly. The island is close to a newly discovered oilfield. Canadian and Danish gunboats have fired at each other.

The caribou herds have almost disappeared from the Arctic. The many new roads and pipelines, which link the Arctic oil wells with the rest of the world, have disrupted the annual migration of the herds.

Inuits, who once lived in the Arctic, have been forced to move into the cities, where their traditional hunting skills are worthless and there are no jobs for them.

Melting on Greenland

The Greenland ice cap covers the whole of the island except around the coast. The ice cap is not melting as fast as the Arctic sea ice, but in 2010, scientists were alarmed because they found that some parts of it are melting much faster than expected. When land ice melts, extra water pours into the ocean. Sea ice, however, is already seawater, and so does not add extra water when it melts.

A production line for icebergs

Ice caps made of land ice are called **glaciers**. A glacier slides slowly downhill and creeps across the land toward the sea. Where it reaches the coast, huge chunks of ice break off and float away as icebergs. In the past, new ice, made by snow falling in the center of Greenland, made up for the ice lost in icebergs.

Sea ice is flat, but icebergs produced by glaciers are tall and rugged. They are made of freshwater and float in the salty ocean.

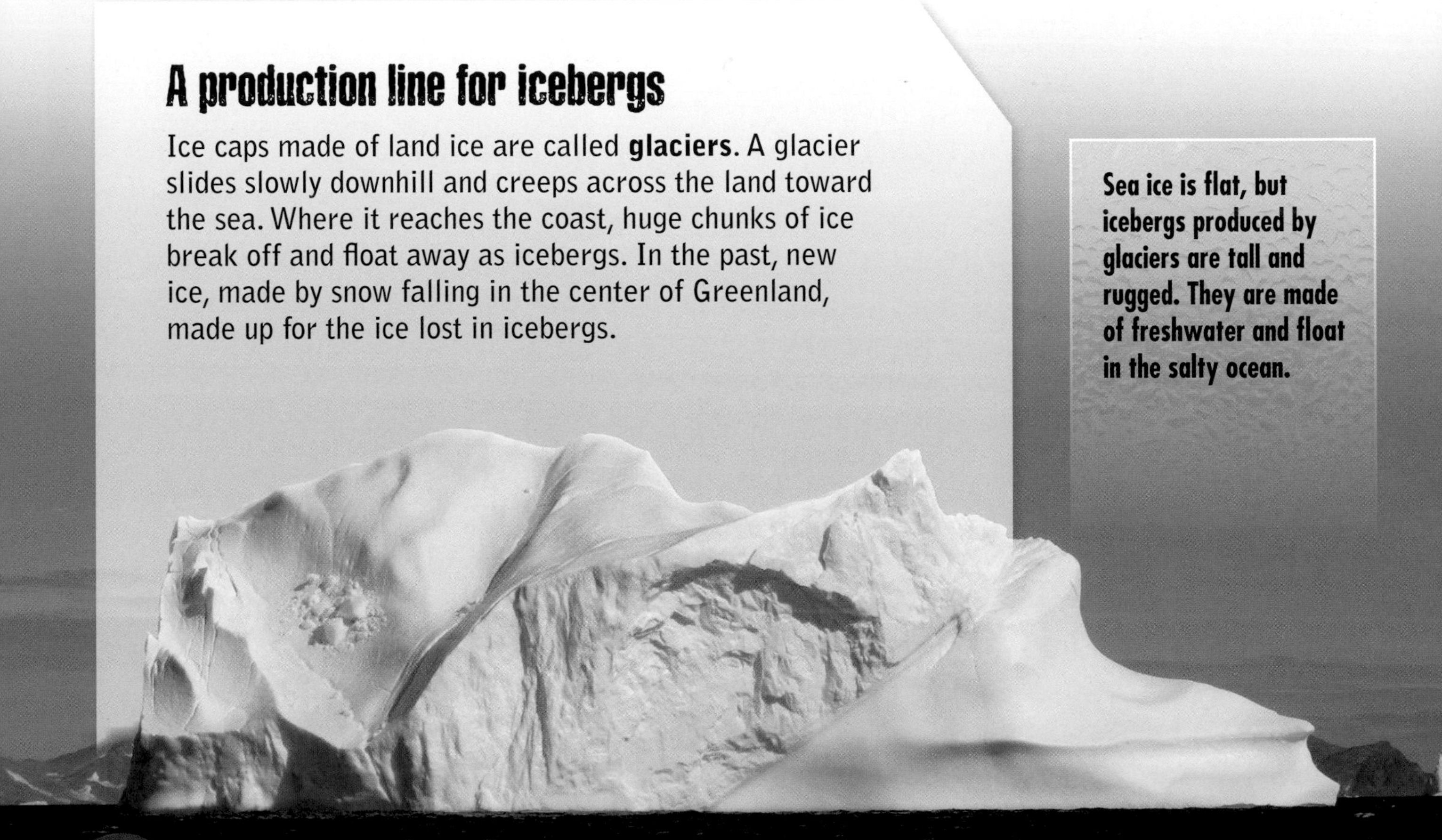

Why are icebergs getting bigger?

Scientists have discovered that the glaciers are moving faster than before. They think that this is because melted ice is gathering under the glacier, making it slide more easily. Faster moving glaciers are producing more and bigger icebergs. In 2010, the biggest Arctic iceberg in 50 years measured 160 square miles (260 sq km).

What happens next?

⚠ Scientists used to think it would take 1,000 years for Greenland's ice cap to melt completely. However, if global warming continues unchecked, scientists predict that the ice sheet could disappear in 200 or 300 years. "The point of no return," however, will come much sooner. Scientists calculate that if global warming increases by just more than one degree, total meltdown on Greenland will be unstoppable.

A glacier is a river of ice that flows so slowly you cannot usually see it move. When it reaches the sea, however, the front of the glacier breaks off and floats away.

Where the Water Goes

The Greenland ice cap is shrinking. Up to 110 billion tons (100 billion t) of ice crash into the sea every year. The melted ice is one reason why the level of the sea is rising. It rose by 6.7 inches (17 cm) between 1900 and 2000, and has risen by more than 1.4 inches (3.5 cm) since 2000. However, **meltwater** is not the only cause of rising sea levels.

What happens when the sea becomes warmer?

About 80 percent of global warming is absorbed by the sea. As the sea warms up, it expands, which pushes up the sea level. Scientists now calculate that the sea will rise by more than a metre by 2100. Even a small rise in sea level can do a lot of damage. Low-lying islands and coasts are already being flooded.

Sea floods

Tuvalu is a low, flat island in the Pacific Ocean. It is thousands of miles away from Greenland, but it is on the front line of rising sea levels. At high tide, seawater now covers the road around the coast. Inland, salty water bubbles up through the ground, poisoning freshwater supplies and farm crops.

Many tropical islands, such as the Maldives in the Indian Ocean, are low and flat. As sea levels rise, many islands are beginning to disappear below the water.

ON THE EDGE

Warmer seas are damaging **coral reefs**. So many kinds of sea creatures live around coral reefs, they have been called the "rainforest of the seas." Coral reefs are fragile. If the sea becomes too warm, the corals lose their color. This is called **bleaching**. If the bleaching lasts longer than a few months, the coral dies. When the coral dies, so too do the animals that live there.

This piece of coral has become bleached because the seawater around it is too warm for it. Fish rely on coral and when the coral dies, they die, too.

Catastrophic Floods

Global warming brings extreme weather. Since 2000, storms and floods have become more common. Some are directly linked to melting ice. Meltwater from high mountains causes rivers to flood inland. At the coast, severe hurricanes bring huge waves and high seas. When they combine with rising sea levels, the result is devastating.

What happens when a mountain glacier melts?

High mountains are covered by glaciers, many of which are melting and shrinking. Meltwater pours down the mountainsides, into the rivers on the plains below. If a river cannot hold the extra water, it floods onto the surrounding land. Some meltwater forms lakes in the mountains. When a lake becomes too big, however, the dam bursts, flooding the valleys below.

In 2010, rain poured down the mountains along the border between Thailand and Cambodia and flooded farmland and homes. The streets were waist-deep in water.

In 2005, water from Lake Pontchartrain flooded through canals into the city of New Orleans. Now, new floodgates protect the city. When the water becomes dangerously high, the gates are lowered to keep the water in the lake.

Destroyed by flood

A flood can be catastrophic. It drowns people and farm animals. It washes away homes and destroys food crops, leaving the survivors with nothing. Some governments try to protect communities from floods. They build sea walls and high banks along riversides. Many countries cannot afford to do this, and even rich countries cannot protect their entire coastlines and riverbanks.

Number Crunching

You don't have to live on a small island to be threatened by floods and rising sea levels. Billions of people live near the sea:

Nearly a quarter (23 percent) of the world's population now lives on or near the coast.

Ten of the 16 biggest cities in the world are fewer than 60 miles (100 km) from the sea.

In Australia, nearly 9 in 10 people live within 30 miles (50 km) of the coast.

The Great Floods: Earth 2050

It is 2050. Global warming has continued faster than predicted. The Greenland ice cap is melting fast and sea levels are rising. People and industries are still burning fossil fuels, while billions of tons of greenhouse gases, stored in the permafrost for millions of years, are being released as the icy ground melts.

Severe floods are becoming so common that it is impossible for governments to protect every town and city with floodgates. Here, a wall of sandbags has been built across the Chao Praya river in Thailand to hold back the water.

Consequences

The consequences are plain to see. This year—2050—six category-5 hurricanes battered the Caribbean and the southern states of the United States. Many islands in the Pacific Ocean and the Indian Ocean have already disappeared beneath the waves. Severe storms have caused floods in Bangladesh, Burma, and Australia.

Crops are failing all over the world. This means that food prices are rocketing.

WHERE WILL YOU BE IN 2050? IT'S YOUR FUTURE!

NEWS HEADLINES

In southern Asia, millions of families have been forced from their homes by the worst flood in several years. Their land is destroyed and they are moving inland, but the land there is already overcrowded. Where will the flood refugees go?

Flood defenses along the Belgium coast have failed. Homes and fields up to several miles from the coast are deep in water.

The state of Florida is shrinking! Storms and rising sea levels have eaten away much of the coast. Even Miami, with its expensive sea walls, cannot keep out the waves. Many inhabitants are leaving the city to resettle elsewhere.

The last remaining island of Kiribati in the Pacific Ocean has disappeared below the rising ocean. Most of the islanders now live in New Zealand, where they have formed a government in **exile**.

Food prices will double yet again this year. Almost the entire wheat crop in the United States has been lost to floods and drought. First came the Mississippi-Missouri flood, followed by the worst drought of the century.

A Mini Ice Age?

Global warming brings changes in climates as well as extreme weather. Scientists can predict general trends but they cannot say exactly what will happen or when it will happen. Some scientists think that global warming could make countries on both sides of the North Atlantic colder—much colder! Temperatures there could drop by 40 to 50° Fahrenheit (5 to 10° C), while the rest of the world becomes hotter.

How can global warming make some places colder?

If the Gulf Stream stops flowing, winters in Britain and Western Europe could become as cold as those in Russia are now.

The Gulf Stream

The Gulf Stream is an **ocean current** that brings warm water from the Caribbean Sea across the Atlantic Ocean to Western Europe. It gives countries around the edge of the northeast Atlantic a milder climate than places in western Canada, which are the same distance from the North Pole. In Britain, for example, it stops the weather from getting very cold in winter.

ON THE EDGE

Western Britain probably benefits most from the Gulf Stream. It has so little frost in winter that palm trees and other tropical plants grow in northwest Scotland. If the Gulf Stream stopped, these trees would be wiped out and sea animals, such as basking sharks and sea horses, would die.

Palm trees normally grow in the tropics, but these ones are growing in Devon in Britain. The warm water of the Gulf Stream keeps the weather on the west coast mild.

Turning off the heat

Some scientists think that the Gulf Stream could stop flowing as a result of global warming. As melting glaciers add extra freshwater to the North Atlantic, the ocean is becoming slightly less salty. At present, cold saltwater near the Arctic sinks, pulling the current of warm surface water northward. The Gulf Stream stopped about 13,000 years ago, after the end of the last ice age, when vast melting glaciers diluted the sea. Could it happen again?

The Big Freeze: Northwest Europe 2075

It is 2075. The Gulf Stream has stopped flowing, so, while most of the world swelters, people in Western Europe are shivering. The climate there is like that of Canada or Siberia was in 2013—more than 60 years ago. Scientists say that this mini ice age could last 100 years.

Europe and North Africa are blanketed in snow in winter.

Consequences

Summers are hot but very short. Winters are long and freezing. Farming continues, but farmers grow fewer types of crops and concentrate on those such as oats, barley, and turnips, which grow in colder conditions. More energy than ever before is being used to heat homes, offices, and other buildings. Much of this energy still comes from the burning of fossil fuels. The continued burning of fossil fuels means that global warming is now out of control.

NEWS HEADLINES

Blizzards are sweeping across Europe into North Africa. Last winter, nearly a million old and vulnerable people died of cold because they could not afford to heat their homes.

Electricity companies in Britain and France are struggling to provide enough electricity. They warn that there will be electricity blackouts again this winter.

Ice floes— lumps of sea ice—have been seen in the North Sea. They are much farther south than ever before and are a hazard to shipping.

Villagers in Wales claim that a polar bear was seen raiding a dustbin. Has it come from a zoo or from the wild? Some people argue that hungry polar bears are dangerous and should be shot. Other people say that we should protect all Arctic animals.

In this new ice age, cities such as Madrid, London (shown here), and Rome are deep in snow for most of the winter. People find it hard to keep warm.

WHERE WILL YOU BE IN 2075? IT'S YOUR FUTURE!

Antarctica: The Big One

Antarctica is as large as the United States and Mexico combined and contains about 90 percent of the world's ice. The ice shelves around Antarctica have been losing millions of tons of ice every year since 2002. However, there is so much ice locked up on Antarctica it would take hundreds or even thousands of years to melt completely. If it did all melt, sea levels would rise by an overwhelming 200 feet (60 m), drowning cities and land on coasts around the world.

Ice shelves are thick areas of ice that float in the sea at the end of glaciers. In 2002, the Larsen B ice shelf collapsed and 550 billion tons (500 billion t) of ice broke up to become icebergs.

Where is the Antarctic ice cap melting?

An ice shelf is an area of thick ice at the end of a glacier. There are ice shelves up to 3,300 feet (1,000 m) thick around nearly half of the Antarctic coast. In summer, chunks of ice from the edge of an ice shelf break off and float away as large, flat icebergs and this is now happening much faster. Some ice shelves have completely collapsed. This worries environmentalists because, once the ice shelf has gone, there is nothing to stop the glacier sliding into the Southern Ocean.

Melting ice shelves threaten the lives of animals such as penguins, who will struggle to find food for themselves and their young.

What happens next?

As ice shelves are lost, Antarctica's many glaciers will slip into the sea, adding freshwater to ever-rising sea levels.

⚠ The melting of the ice shelves will damage sea life, particularly the tiny **krill**, which live under the ice. Blue whales, seals, and penguins and other Antarctic wildlife feed mainly on krill. The number of krill has already dropped by 80 percent, which scientists think is linked to the melting ice shelves. Further losses will endanger animals that feed on them, such as penguins.

Four Degrees Hotter: Earth 2100

It is 2100. The average temperature of the world is now 40° Fahrenheit (4° C) warmer than it was in the 1850s, when humans started burning large amounts of fossil fuels. The rise in temperature is not evenly spread across the world, but is instead concentrated on the land, particularly the land around the Arctic.

Much of Iran is semi-desert. People here know how to use water carefully to grow some crops and sustain life.

Consequences

Many areas of the world are becoming uninhabitable. Rising sea levels and worsening storms have caused devastating coastal floods. In 2000, 600 million people lived fewer than 33 feet (10 m) above sea level. Now, in 2100, most of these people have left the coast and crowded inland. Drought and rising sea levels have destroyed vast areas of farmland. Competition for limited supplies of freshwater has led to wars between nations badly hit by drought.

Even as land around the coast is flooded, deserts inland are becoming larger. Large areas of desert are becoming as barren as the Sahara.

Desalination plants turns salty seawater into drinkable freshwater. Although they are expensive to build and run, they have become vital as supplies of natural freshwater become scarce.

NEWS HEADLINES

Cities along the eastern coast of the United States, from New York to Houston are struggling to recover from the catastrophic floods caused by hurricanes this year.

Six expensive new factories to produce drinking water from saltwater have been built in Greece this year. Such desalination plants are now a common sight in drought-stricken nations, particularly in Australia, the United States, and the Middle East.

Thousands of desperate people from southern Asia are pleading with rich countries to take them in. Many want to live in the tundra. This land was once an empty wilderness, but the warmer climate has made it possible to farm there.

Africa and southern Asia are particularly badly affected by drought, famine, and increasing deserts.

Can We Survive?

The glimpses into the future described in this book assume that people and governments do nothing to stop the rise in global warming. To avoid the worst outcomes, scientists warn that global warming needs to be limited to a rise of 3.6° Fahrenheit (2° C) this century. Otherwise, experts predict that the outcome could be catastrophic for millions of people.

Solar power stations can be built almost anywhere, from deserts to mountains. All they need is lots of sunlight to produce clean electricity with no greenhouse gas emissions.

What can we do to prevent disaster?

Most scientists and environmentalists agree that if we are to limit global warming, we have to stop burning fossil fuels. Many individual people already do what they can. Some try to avoid traveling by air and by car. Others have **solar panels** to generate electricity and they **insulate** their homes to reduce the amount of electricity they use. Nevertheless, individuals alone cannot solve the problem.

Environmental groups want governments to take the lead in limiting global warming. For example, they press governments to guarantee that they will reduce the amount of greenhouse gases each country produces. Most governments, however, will not take action unless all governments do the same. As politicians and governments argue, the ice caps melt.

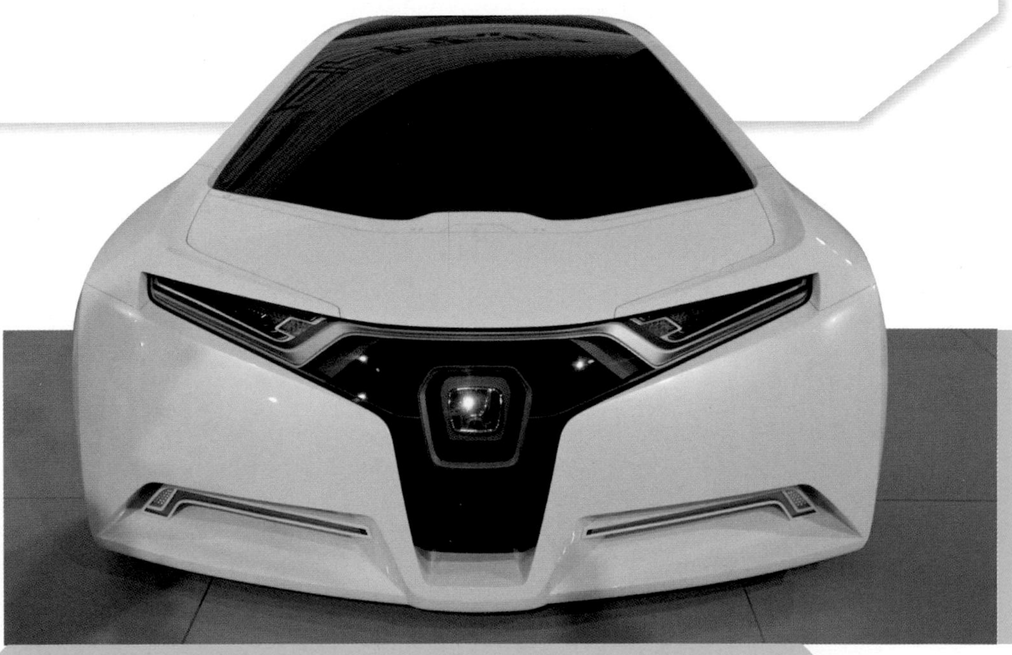

Cars such as this one could become popular in the future. This sports car uses a fuel cell to produce electricity to power its electric motor.

ON THE EDGE

Scientists say that there is still time to limit global warming this century to 3.6° (2° C), but we do not have long. The technology exists to replace fossil fuels with other forms of energy. Fuel cells, for example, produce electricity from hydrogen and are already used in some buses. Such alternative technology is still expensive, however. It would become cheaper if governments invested more money in it.

Glossary

bleaching turning white

caribou large reindeer that live in North America. Inuits rely on caribou for food and clothes

category-5 hurricanes the strongest hurricanes, with winds more than 155 mph (249 km/h)

climate type of weather a place normally gets at different times of the year

coral reefs ridges of coral built by billions of tiny shellfish called polyps

desalination plant factory that produces freshwater from saltwater

environmentalists people who work to protect the environment

exile when a person or people are unable to return to their native land

fossil fuels fuels, particularly oil, coal, and natural gas, which formed millions of years ago from the remains of plants and animals

glaciers huge volumes of ice that flow slowly downhill across the land

global warming average increase in temperature at the Earth's surface

greenhouse gases gases such as carbon dioxide and methane in the atmosphere, which trap the Sun's heat and so cause global warming

ice cap large area of thick ice

ice sheet thick ice that covers more than 31,000 square miles (50,000 sq km) of land

ice shelves areas of floating ice that are attached to the land and which block the glaciers behind them from sliding into the ocean

insulate stop heat from entering or leaving

krill very tiny shellfish, like microscopic shrimps

land ice frozen freshwater that rests on land

meltwater ice that has melted to form water

migrate move from one place to another

ocean current steady flow of warmer or colder seawater through the ocean

oil slick mass of oil that has spilled from a tanker or pipeline. Oil slicks pollute the sea and the coast

permafrost land around the Arctic Ocean that is permanently frozen below the surface

pipeline large pipe that takes oil from one place to another

sea ice frozen seawater that floats in the sea

solar panels special panels that use the energy of sunlight to generate electricity. Solar panels do not create greenhouse gases

tundra vast, flat treeless Arctic region where the soil is permanently frozen

uninhabitable unsuitable for living in

Further Information

Books

Climate Change: Can the Earth Cope? Richard Spilsbury, Wayland 2012.

Eco Alert: Climate Change, Rebecca Hunter, Franklin Watts, 2012.

Ecosystems: Climate Change, Peter Benoit, Children's Press, 2011.

Unstable Earth: What Happens If the Ozone Disappears? Mary Colson, Smart Apple Media, 2015.

Unstable Earth: What Happens If the Rain Forests Disappear? Mary Colson, Smart Apple Media, 2015.

Unstable Earth: What Happens If We Overfish the Oceans? Angela Royston, Smart Apple Media, 2015.

Websites

www.epa.gov/climatechange/kids/impacts/signs/index.html
From this screen on the United States Environmental Protection Agency's website for children, you can find out about the effects of shrinking sea ice, melting glaciers, rising sea levels, and much more.

ga.water.usgs.gov/edu/earthglacier.html
Check out this website that gives facts and figures about the ice caps and how they have changed over thousands of years.

insidc.org/cryosphere/quickfacts/index.html
The National Snow and Ice Data Center gives quick facts about each of the different kinds of ice, including ice sheets and icebergs.

Index